IS-702.A: National Incident Management System (NIMS) Public Information Systems

By

Fema

10/31/2013

Lesson 1: Course Overview

Course Welcome

The public information component described in the National Incident Management System (NIMS) is designed to effectively manage public information at an incident, regardless of the size and complexity of the situation or the number of entities involved in the response.

The goal of this course is to facilitate NIMS implementation by providing you with the basic information and tools you will need to apply NIMS public information best practices and protocols during incident management.

Our Goal: An Informed Public

Disaster may strike at any time and any place. Whether caused by the forces of nature or precipitated by the actions of man, disaster can take lives and destroy property. Our best defense against this devastation is an informed public. This course introduces you to the systems used to deliver the right information to the right people at the right time. Information helps empower people to make effective decisions.

For Experienced PIOs . . .

This course is designed for experienced Public Information Officers (PIOs). It will touch on the fundamentals of effective public information programs, but only to illustrate or provide examples for the details of the NIMS public information element.

Those who want more complete coverage of public information in the emergency management environment should go to http://www.training.fema.gov/EMIWeb/Programs/ to learn more about the Basic Public Information Officers Course (G-290), which is taught by the States, and the Advanced Public Information Officers Course (E-388), which is taught at the Emergency Management Institute (EMI).

Course Objectives

At the conclusion of this course, you should be able to:

- Define the NIMS public information element including onsite operations, the Joint Information System (JIS), and the Joint Information Center (JIC), and how they relate to each other.
- Describe the JIS/JIC process of gathering, verifying, coordinating, and disseminating information by public information and incident management personnel.
- Identify each agency involved in given emergency situations and the role of each in the JIS to ensure appropriate situational awareness information is communicated to the public.
- Define key terms related to NIMS public information and its relationship to Multiagency Coordination (MAC) Systems and the field.
- Identify typical public information resource requirements.

Lesson Overview

This first lesson provides a brief overview of the National Incident Management System (NIMS) and the public information element.

What Is NIMS?

The National Incident Management System (NIMS) provides the foundation needed to ensure that we can work together when our communities and the Nation need us the most.

Each day communities respond to numerous emergencies. Most often, these incidents are managed effectively at the local level.

However, there are some incidents that may require a collaborative approach that includes personnel from:

- Multiple jurisdictions,
- A combination of specialties or disciplines,
- Several levels of government,
- Nongovernmental organizations, and
- The private sector.

The National Incident Management System, or NIMS, provides the foundation needed to ensure that we can work together when our communities and the Nation need us the most.

NIMS integrates best practices into a comprehensive, standardized framework that is flexible enough to be applicable across the full spectrum of potential incidents, regardless of cause, size, location, or complexity.

Using NIMS allows us to work together to prepare for, prevent, respond to, recover from, and mitigate the effects of incidents.

Homeland Security Presidential Directives

- HSPD-5 identified steps for improved coordination in response to incidents. It requires the Department of Homeland Security (DHS) to coordinate with other Federal departments and agencies and State, local, and tribal governments to establish a National Response Framework (NRF) and a National Incident Management System (NIMS).
- HSPD-8 directed DHS to lead a national initiative to develop a National Preparedness System-a common, unified approach to "strengthen the preparedness of the United States to prevent and respond to threatened or actual domestic terrorist attacks, major disasters, and other emergencies." ([PPD-8] "replaces Homeland Security Presidential Directive (HSPD)-8 (National Preparedness), issued December 17, 2003, and HSPD-8 Annex I (National Planning), issued December 4, 2007, which are hereby rescinded, except for paragraph 44 of HSPD-8 Annex I. Individual plans developed under HSPD-8 and Annex I remain in effect until rescinded or otherwise replaced." Source PPD-8 page 5 paragraph 5)

NIMS and NRF

NIMS provides a systematic, proactive approach to guide departments and agencies at all levels of government, nongovernmental organizations, and the private sector to work seamlessly to prevent, protect against, respond to, recover from, and mitigate the effects of incidents, regardless of cause, size, location, or complexity, in order to reduce the loss of life and property and harm to the environment.

The NRF is a guide to how the Nation conducts all-hazards response — from the smallest incident to the largest catastrophe. This key document establishes a comprehensive, national, all-hazards approach to domestic incident response. The Framework identifies the key response principles, roles, and structures that organize national response. It describes how communities, States, the Federal Government, and private-sector and nongovernmental partners apply these principles for a coordinated, effective national response.

NIMS Components

NIMS is much more than just using the Incident Command System (ICS) or an organization chart.
NIMS is a consistent, nationwide, systematic approach that includes the following components:

Preparedness

Actions taken to plan, organize, equip, train, and exercise to build and sustain the capabilities necessary to prevent, protect against, mitigate the effects of, respond to, and recover from those threats that pose the greatest risk. Within NIMS, preparedness focuses on the following elements: planning; procedures and protocols; training and exercises; personnel qualifications, licensure, and certification; and equipment certification.

Communications and Information Management

Emergency management and incident response activities rely on communications and information systems that provide a common operating picture to all command and coordination sites. NIMS describes the requirements necessary for a standardized framework for communications and emphasizes the need for a common operating picture. This component is based on the concepts of interoperability, reliability, scalability, and portability, as well as the resiliency and redundancy of communications and information systems.

Resource Management

Resources (such as personnel, equipment, or supplies) are needed to support critical incident objectives. The flow of resources must be fluid and adaptable to the requirements of the incident. NIMS defines standardized mechanisms and establishes the resource management process to identify requirements, order and acquire, mobilize, track and report, recover and demobilize, reimburse, and inventory resources.

Command and Management

The Command and Management component of NIMS is designed to enable effective and efficient incident management and coordination by providing a flexible, standardized incident management structure. The structure is based on three key organizational constructs: the Incident Command System (ICS), Multiagency Coordination (MAC) Systems, and Public Information.

Ongoing Management and Maintenance

Within the auspices of Ongoing Management and Maintenance, there are two
components: the National Integration Center (NIC) and Supporting Technologies.

Command and Management Elements

The NIMS Command and Management component facilitates incident management. This
component includes the following elements: Incident Command System, Multiagency
Coordination Systems, and Public Information.

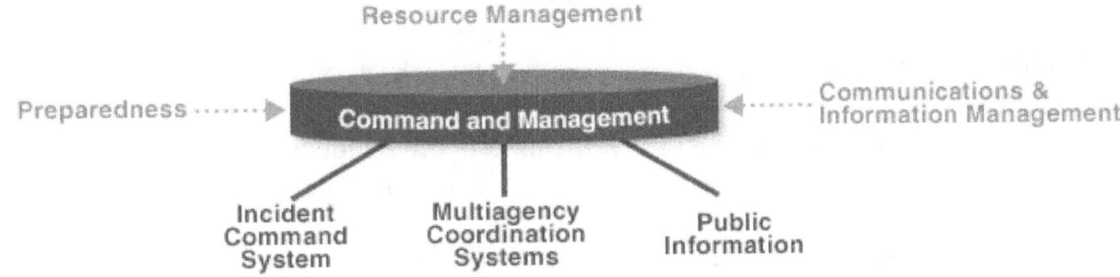

NIMS Definition of Public Information

As defined in NIMS, public
information consists of the
processes, procedures, and systems
for communicating timely,
accurate, and accessible
information on:

- An incident's cause, size,
  and current situation;
- Resources committed; and
- Other matters of general
  interest to the public,
  responders, and additional
  stakeholders (both directly
  affected and indirectly
  affected).

Public Information

Public information, education strategies, and communications plans help ensure that numerous audiences receive timely, consistent messages about:

- Lifesaving measures.
- Evacuation routes.
- Threat and alert system notices.
- Other public safety information.

Public Information Principles

NIMS public information is based on the following three basic principles:

- The Public Information Officer (PIO) supports the Incident Command.
- Public information functions must be coordinated and integrated across jurisdictions and across functional agencies; among Federal, State, local, and tribal partners; and with private-sector and nongovernmental organizations.
- Organizations participating in public information coordination retain their independence.

Lesson 2:

NIMS Public Information Overview

Lesson Overview

This lesson will describe the principles and system components that comprise the NIMS public information element. At the end of this lesson, you should be able to:

- Describe the mission of public information in relation to incident management.
- Describe the role of the Public Information Officer (PIO) in incident management.
- Describe how the NIMS public information element accommodates functionality at single and multiple levels of government, and across jurisdictional and agency lines.

NIMS Public Information

NIMS public information is based on the lessons learned by PIOs responding to countless incidents in communities throughout the Nation.

Experienced PIOs will not be surprised by what they read in the section of NIMS that deals with public information. The principles, system components, and procedures described in that document acknowledge and reinforce what has been used successfully in the field during incidents regardless of size or complexity.

Public Information Mission During an Incident

The public information mission during an incident is to get accurate, understandable information to the public in a timely manner so people can take action to save lives and minimize damage to property.

NIMS public information procedures and protocols support this mission.

NIMS Public Information Principles

As mentioned in the previous lesson, NIMS public information is based on the following principles:

1. The PIO supports the Incident Command.
2. Public information functions must be coordinated and integrated across jurisdictions and functional agencies; among Federal, State, local, and tribal partners; and with private-sector and nongovernmental organizations, such as the American Red Cross.
3. Organizations participating in incident management retain their independence.

Let's take a closer look at the first principle—the role of the PIO in support of Incident Command.

Who Is the Public Information Officer?

When an incident occurs, the relevant agencies or departments are dispatched to the scene. The lead agency assumes Incident Command and a PIO is designated. Usually this person is a full-time PIO whose role in an incident has been predetermined in emergency plans and standard operating procedures.

Role of the Public Information Officer

Under the Incident Command System (ICS)—the system that defines the operating characteristics, management components, and organizational structure under NIMS—the PIO is a key staff member supporting the Incident Command structure. The PIO advises and represents the Incident Command on all public information matters relating to the management of the incident.

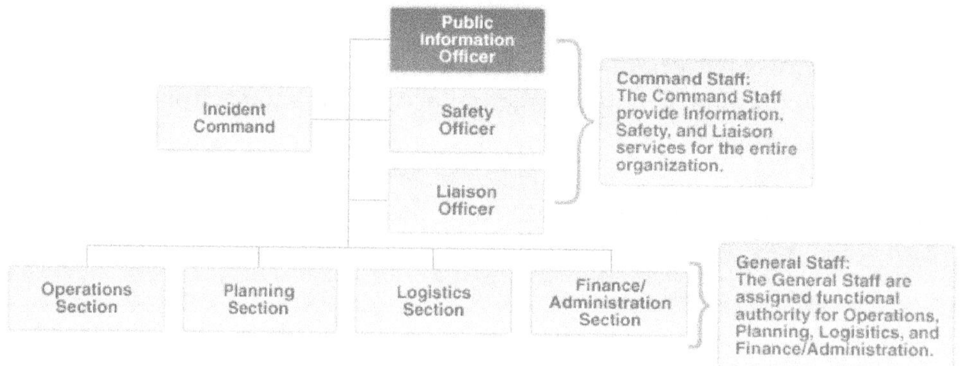

Basic PIO Responsibilities

The Public Information Officer supports the incident command structure as a member of the Command Staff. PIOs are able to create coordinated and consistent messages by collaborating to:

- Identify key information that needs to be communicated to the public.
- Craft messages conveying key information that are clear and easily understood by all, including those with access and functional needs.
- Prioritize messages to ensure timely delivery of information without overwhelming the audience.
- Verify accuracy of information through appropriate channels.
- Disseminate messages using the most effective means available.

Activating the Joint Information System

The PIO is responsible for knowing when and how to activate the Joint Information System (JIS). The JIS is the method of operating during an incident that allows multiple PIOs to coordinate information and integrate messages to avoid confusing the public.

Scalable System

The role of the PIO remains basically the same under NIMS, regardless of the type and size of the event. NIMS allows for flexibility and scalability to meet the needs of the incident. Let's look at how NIMS public information operates in three different types of incidents.

Regional Event—Large Accident

NIMS is followed when the characteristics of an event are complex or require coordination somewhat beyond normal, day-to-day working relationships. For example, a large accident on a major highway crossing several jurisdictions would require coordination among the affected jurisdictions and several departments (i.e., fire, police, transportation). A flood or other natural disaster affecting several jurisdictions would also require coordination among the localities as well as regional or State entities.

The NIMS public information element is also crucial when the incident is dynamic or when the focus and primary information source will change from one agency or department to another. For example, imagine that a number of children become sick at school. Emergency Medical Services (EMS) is called to the scene and is the initial information source. It soon becomes evident that the children are suffering from a highly contagious strain of influenza, which begins showing up in people throughout the community. Public Health gets involved and victims are quarantined at the school. The primary information source has shifted to the Public Health agency and the list of affected jurisdictions and departments has expanded. In these multijurisdiction, multidepartment events, media coverage may include State or regional as well as local news media.

EOC Activated

NIMS defines multiagency coordination (MAC) as a system that provides the architecture to support coordination for incident prioritization, critical resource allocation, communications systems integration, and information coordination. MAC Systems assist agencies and organizations responding to an incident. MAC System elements include facilities, equipment, personnel, procedures, and communications. A MAC System can be as simple as a teleconference among affected jurisdictions and departments. At other times it may include the on-scene command structure and responders as well as other components of multiagency coordination (e.g., resource coordination centers, coordination entities, Emergency Operations Centers (EOCs), and dispatch).

If multiple local agencies are involved, a local EOC may be opened. If multiple jurisdictions and/or State agencies are involved, a State EOC also may be opened. Likewise, Federal coordination may be called for, depending upon the nature of the incident.

When an EOC is activated, a Joint Information Center (JIC) (described in Lesson 5) will be established in proximity to the EOC to provide a base of operation for the public information function. At this point, the JIC supports the on-scene PIO and may assume primary responsibility for public information, with the PIOs on the scene serving as field PIOs. Coverage will include local, State, regional, and perhaps national news media.

Incident Requiring National Coordination

In incidents requiring national coordination, the Federal Government works in concert with State, local, and tribal governments and the private sector to ensure a coordinated, effective national response.

Lesson 3: Joint Information System Concept

Lesson Overview

This lesson will describe how NIMS addresses coordination of public information. At the end of this lesson, you should be able to:

- Define the Joint Information System (JIS) relative to NIMS.
- Describe how the JIS coordinates public information efforts among jurisdictions and agencies.
- Describe how the JIS allows entities to convey their unique information to the public while working collectively to develop and disseminate accurate, coordinated, and unified messages.
- Describe how the philosophy of "getting the right information to the right people at the right time so they can make the right decisions" defines the mission of public information during incident management.
- Identify agencies and organizations that may be part of the JIS.

Principle of Coordination and Integration

NIMS public information is coordinated and integrated across jurisdictions and functional agencies; among Federal, State, local, and tribal partners; and with private-sector entities and nongovernmental organizations.

The Joint Information System is the structure for ensuring that PIO functions are coordinated and integrated.

Joint Information System

The Joint Information System (JIS):

- Provides the mechanism to organize, integrate, and coordinate information to ensure timely, accurate, accessible, and consistent messaging across multiple jurisdictions and/or disciplines with nongovernmental organizations and the private sector.

- Includes the plans, protocols, procedures, and structures used to provide public information.

Federal, State, tribal, territorial, regional, or local Public Information Officers and established Joint Information Centers (JICs) are critical supporting elements of the JIS.

Joint Information Center

The Joint Information Center (JIC) is:

- A central location that facilitates operation of the Joint Information System.
- A location where personnel with public information responsibilities perform critical emergency information functions, crisis communications, and public affairs functions.

JICs may be established at various levels of government or at incident sites, or can be components of Multiagency Coordination (MAC) Systems (e.g., MAC Groups or EOCs). A single JIC location is preferable, but the system is flexible and adaptable enough to accommodate virtual or multiple JIC locations, as required.

Voices of Experience

Melinda Kletzok: Depending on the incident a whole bunch of people can get involved. If it's a flood you are going to be working with social service agencies, with the police, with fire, with the hospitals, with the gamut, so that's why it's so important to have an actual system because you get so many agencies involved depending on what your incident is.

Christopher Kramer: The public doesn't want to see agencies argue and fight, they want to see a solid response effort that's going to allow them to get back to their lives as quickly as possible and get back to their daily routines.

Jim Bunstock: I think it boils down to communication. It's just like any other relationship: without good communication there is no singleness of purpose. You are working at cross purposes.

How the Joint Information System Operates

In an emergency, the JIS provides the mechanism for integrating public information activities to ensure coordinated and consistent message development, verification, and dissemination. The JIS can be:

- As simple as two PIOs talking on the phone about an incident that involves both of their agencies.
- A PIO at the Emergency Operations Center (EOC) talking to a PIO at the site of the incident.
- PIOs from several departments working together at a single location.
- Many PIOs from many agencies working from several locations—all working together to ensure clear and accurate information is being delivered to the public.

Joint Information System (JIS): Speaking With One Voice

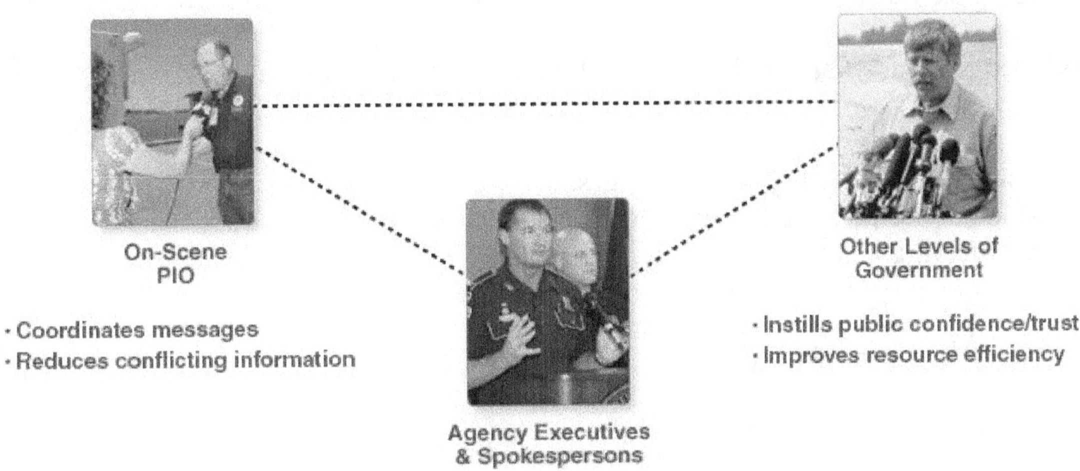

Coordinated and Consistent Messages

Through the JIS, PIOs are able to create coordinated and consistent messages by collaborating to:

- Identify key information that needs to be communicated to the public.
- Craft messages that convey key information, and are clear and easily understood.
- Prioritize messages to ensure timely delivery of information without overwhelming the audience.

- Verify accuracy of information through appropriate channels, including Incident Command and relevant agencies and program areas.
- Disseminate messages using the most effective means available.

Principle of Autonomy

The JIS also supports the third principle under the NIMS public information element. Organizations participating in incident management retain their autonomy.

The departments, agencies, organizations, or jurisdictions that contribute to the JIS do not lose their individual identities or responsibility for their own programs or policies.

Getting It Right

Simply stated, the public information mission during an incident is to get the right information to the right people at the right time so they can make the right decisions.

The JIS helps PIOs accomplish this mission by facilitating coordination. PIOs also follow specific strategies to avoid conflicting messages, such as:

- Focusing on one or two key messages.
- Using pre-scripted messages, as appropriate.
- Using talking points.
- Designating spokesperson(s) for media interviews.
- Speaking about one's own program—not others' programs.

Lesson 4: Pre-Incident Activities

Lesson Overview

This lesson will focus on those things an organization must do **before** an incident occurs in order to effectively manage public information responsibilities. At the end of this lesson, you should be able to:

- Describe the staffing and skills necessary to support effective public information.
- Describe the equipment and other resources needed for effective public information during an incident.
- Identify partners who contribute to public information during an incident and who should be involved in planning.
- Identify the topics to include in plans and procedures necessary for effective public information.
- Apply the concepts in this lesson to assess your public information staffing, resources, and planning.

Who and What Do You Need?

Start by looking at what you will need in order to perform effectively in an incident. Remember, the Public Information Officer (PIO) is responsible for:

- Responding to inquiries from the news media and the public.
- Monitoring the news media to detect and correct misinformation and to identify emerging trends or issues.
- Advising Incident Command on public information issues and advocating for the community to ensure their public information needs are met.
- Managing the release of emergency public information and warnings.
- Coordinating, clearing with appropriate authorities, and disseminating accurate and timely information related to the incident.

Staffing an Incident

Staffing during an incident can be a challenge for many public information operations. A one-person shop cannot provide 24/7 coverage or be at two places—such as the incident site and the EOC—at the same time.

The Joint Information System (JIS) can offer opportunities for staffing. You may be able to tap the skills and staff of other organizations involved in the incident, but other organizations are only one source of supplemental staff.

Voices of Experience

Melinda Kletzok: Staffing during an incident can become a real challenge and sometimes you have to think outside the box. Basically, anybody who can write, you are looking for people who might be a professor at the local university if you have one, students who are good writers can help, people who work in public relations.

Bill Peat: We bring in people from other State agencies sometimes to help us out, people that are familiar with that position, people that have either worked there before or work in other agencies' public information offices.

Jim Bunstock: I bring in public information officers from other State agencies. We have a cadre of people who have agreed to relocate to the JIC whenever necessary and we do some cross training so that we bring people up to speed in different areas and we're able to do multi-shift staffing.

Methods for Supplementing Staff

Methods for supplementing regular PIO staff during emergencies include:

- Using PIOs "on loan" from other departments or agencies.
- Hiring part- or full-time staff with public information expertise.
- Using disaster employees or "on-call" staff with public information expertise.
- Contracting with a public affairs firm for certain functions (for example, Web site maintenance or language translation).
- Acquiring staff through mutual aid and assistance groups.

Authority for Supplementing Staff

Authority to tap other departments or agencies for staff during an incident may be written into law and tied to an emergency declaration (for example, by the Mayor or Governor).

Hiring policies also should be written ahead of time to allow for emergency hiring authority for part- or full-time temporary positions.

In some instances, mutual aid and assistance arrangements or memorandums of understanding (MOUs) will be used.

Important guidelines for supplementing incident staffing include:

- Have agreements to supplement staffing in place **before** the need arises.
- Request help sooner rather than later.

Relationships With the News Media

Developing effective working relationships with the news media is a crucial pre-incident activity.

To get an idea of how to best work with the news media, start by putting yourself in the reporter's shoes. Reporters in all outlets tend to work under time pressures and often are covering multiple stories. If the PIO can serve as the reporter's "helper" in getting accurate, needed information quickly, then the reporter is more likely to be cooperative in getting the PIO's messages out.

Building Relationships

A reporter who understands emergency management and incident command will be better able to comprehend the messages you want to get out to the public.

Likewise, the better you understand the reporter's environment (e.g., print, TV, radio) and each outlet's particular needs, the better able you will be to use the news media as a resource to get information to the public.

Facilities, Equipment, and Supplies

In addition to the people, you also need the tools required for the job. When planning, it is helpful to think of the essentials as well as the supplementary resources (things you can do without, but would like to have).

You should also consider what you need to operate:

- Alone, at the site of the incident or some other location away from your regular work location; and

- With a small or large number of other PIOs at a fixed location, such as a Joint Information Center at an Emergency Operations Center (EOC).

Onsite and On the Go

To respond to an incident, you will need the basic equipment to do the job and it must be portable and ready for rapid deployment. In addition to the basics like paper and pencils, your "go kit" should include technology such as:

- Cell phone (with voice messaging and caller ID; keep spare battery and charger for wall and car; pre-program primary contact numbers).
- Pager (great backup to the cell phone; can work in areas where cell phones won't).
- PDA or handheld device (e.g., iPhone™, BlackBerry®, etc.).
- Camera (with extra storage device and batteries).
- Audio recorder (good for documenting interviews; with extra batteries and tapes if needed).
- Notebook computer (have extra battery; consider features like docking station, wireless network, CD burner).

More Go-Kit Resources

Go kits should include more than just equipment and technology resources. Some other resources to include in your go kit are:

- Contact information for disaster employees and other PIOs who may be called into service.
- Contact information for news media.
- Pre-scripted Emergency Alert System messages, news releases, factsheets, and backgrounders.
- Your "Smart Book." Your own creation, a Smart Book can include any factual information you might be asked, such as population, number of schools, number of hospitals, size and description of geographic or infrastructure features (e.g., size of State park, length of bridge, amount of water in reservoir), etc.

Preparing To Co-Locate PIOs

Remember that a JIS can be one PIO at the scene communicating with other PIOs over the phone. If an incident is of the size or complexity to warrant it, however, an EOC may be activated and the JIS will operate from a Joint Information Center (JIC). (JICs are discussed in detail in Lesson 5.)

Pre-incident activities include planning and preparing to establish a JIC by:

- Establishing a dedicated location where PIOs can work.
- Identifying equipment and supplies—what you need and where you'll get it.
- Wiring the location for phone, Internet access, cable, etc.
- Practicing "morphing" the space into a JIC, as quite often such dedicated spaces are used for other purposes during nonemergency times.

Public Information—Where It Fits

Emergency Operations Plans usually address both common response issues and specific hazards. An effective Emergency Operations Plan will be:

- **Comprehensive:** The plan will include complete response procedures for everyone who has a role in the response.
- **Risk-based:** The plan will address the actual risks facing the jurisdiction.
- **All-hazards in approach:** The plan will apply in any hazardous situation, from lightning strike to terrorist threat.

Public information issues are addressed as an annex to the comprehensive Emergency Operations Plan.

Creating the Public Information Annex

How the Public Information Annex is created is as important as the information it contains. Involving key stakeholders in the planning process helps to ensure that nothing is overlooked.

PIOs from agencies that may be involved in incident response should be part of your planning team.

Components of the Public Information Annex

The Public Information Annex should include such things as:

- Mission

- Organization
- Concept of Operations
- Checklists of Actions (for various stages and types of incidents)

The plan or annex should address specific functions, such as establishing a Public Inquiry Center and activating the Emergency Alert System (EAS). The plan also may include sample news releases or EAS messages.

Lesson 5:

Public Information During the Incident

Lesson Overview

This lesson will focus on the Joint Information Center—the place from which the Joint Information System operates. At the end of this lesson, you should be able to:

- Differentiate between the Joint Information System (JIS) and the Joint Information Center (JIC).
- Describe the Public Information Officer (PIO) function at a command post and a Multiagency Coordination (MAC) entity.
- Describe how the JIC can be configured to support public information for incidents of varying sizes and complexities.
- Describe the basic JIC functional areas and organization.

Review: JIS vs. JIC

Lesson 2 introduced the following concepts:

The **Joint Information System (JIS)** provides a structure and system for:

- Developing and delivering coordinated interagency messages.
- Developing, recommending, and executing public information plans and strategies on behalf of the Incident Commander.
- Advising the Incident Commander concerning public affairs issues.
- Controlling rumors and inaccurate information.

The **Joint Information Center (JIC)** is a physical location used to coordinate:

- Critical emergency information.
- Crisis communications.
- Public affairs functions.

What Is a JIC?

The JIC is a central location to facilitate operation of the JIS during and after an incident. The JIC enhances information coordination, reduces misinformation, and maximizes resources by co-locating Public Information Officers (PIOs) as much as possible.

The JIC isn't the same as the JIS and doesn't replace the JIS. The JIS is a **way** of operating; the JIC is one location **where** the operation takes place.

The next screen illustrates how the JIC fits within the JIS.

Joint Information Center

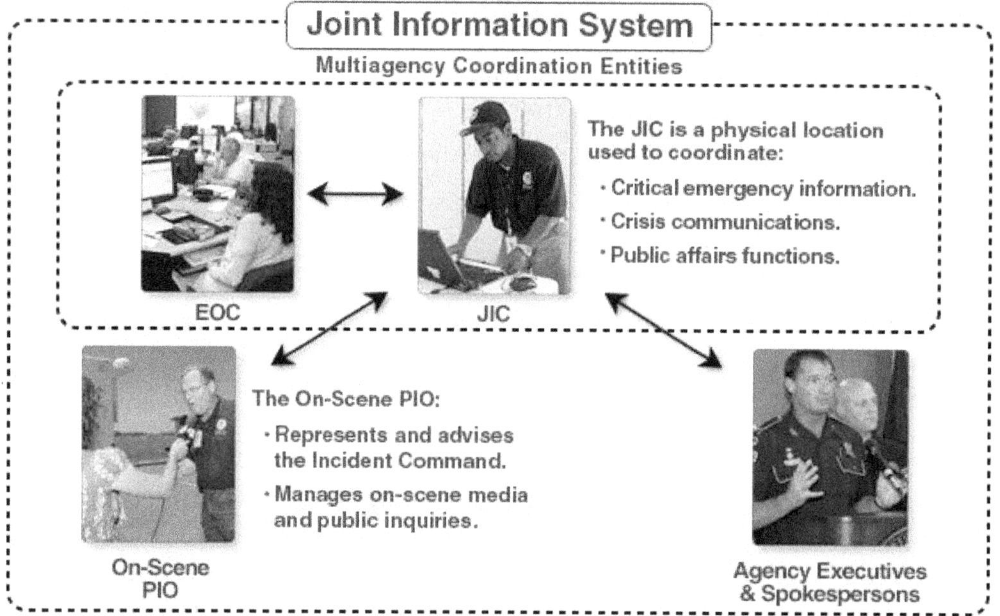

Lessons Learned: Importance of Joint Information Centers

After the September 11, 2001, attack on the Pentagon, the Federal Bureau of Investigation chose not to activate a JIC.

The Arlington County After-Action Report states, "**The failure to establish a JIC proved to be an impediment to the presentation of coordinated, factual, and timely public information.**"

Lessons Learned: Southern California Firestorm 2003

The following findings are from a study commissioned for the Wildland Fire Lessons Learned Center:

- Where a JIC was established, it had a positive effect on the timeliness and quality of the information campaign.
- These incidents received international attention and the need for an information campaign reached a threshold much larger than any one agency could manage effectively. The JIC combined the people and unique strengths of different agencies' public affairs staffs.
- The JIC allowed a unified message to be presented to the public and the media. The JIC could communicate key fire management issues (e.g., the use of air tankers, the need for defensible space) and address these issues proactively through public information while fires held the public's attention.

JIC Characteristics

NIMS describes the following characteristics of a JIC:

- JICs may be established at each level of incident management—local, State, regional, national—as required.
- The JIC includes representatives of each jurisdiction, agency, private-sector entity, and nongovernmental organization involved in incident management activities.
- While co-locating PIOs in a single location is ideal, the response system should accommodate multiple JIC locations when circumstances of the incident require. For example, multiple JICs may be needed for multiple, related incidents or a single, complex incident spanning a wide geographic area or multiple jurisdictions. In other words, every EOC has a JIC.

- Each JIC must have procedures and protocols to communicate and coordinate effectively with other JICs, as well as with other appropriate components of Incident Command.

Benefits of the JIC

Establishing a JIC as part of incident response offers the following benefits:

- **A central working facility** where PIOs can gather. Whether it is a small office, the corner of a command center, or a pre-established facility with multiple phone lines, computers, and media-monitoring resources, a JIC makes coordination easier by bringing PIOs together.
- **Pooled resources.** A JIC offers more access to resources than possible in the field using a go kit.

More Benefits of the JIC

Other benefits of establishing a JIC include the following:

- **Strength in numbers.** When more PIOs are working together there is a greater opportunity to make use of individual PIO talents. PIOs can focus attention on specific activities, rather than having to "do it all."
- **Safety.** Working out of a JIC provides a measure of safety not afforded to PIOs working alone in the field. The JIC is also a central location for families and others to check in and make contact with PIOs working the incident.
- **Recognized source.** The JIC is the recognized source for the news media to get official information.

Voices of Experience

Melinda Kletzok: JICs are one of the best tools to come along for public information. A lot of things happen during an emergency that you are not prepared for but at least you can be prepared for the structure in which to operate.

Christopher Kramer: One of the keys in having successful a Joint Information System and a Joint Information Center is during any type crisis it's important for public information people to kind of check their egos at the door, you've got to work as a team. The primary goal of public information for Joint Information Systems and a Joint Information Center is to get information out to the public so they can make informed, rational decisions to protect their safety and welfare and to do that effectively you need a team approach.

Single vs. Multiple JICs

A single JIC location is preferable, but the system is flexible and adaptable enough to accommodate multiple physical or virtual JIC locations. For example, multiple JICs may be needed for a complex incident spanning a wide geographic area or multiple jurisdictions. In instances when multiple JICs are activated, information must be coordinated among all appropriate JICs; each JIC must have procedures and protocols to communicate and coordinate effectively with one another.

Whenever there are multiple JICs, the final release authority must be the senior command, whether using Unified or Area Command structures. A national JIC may be used when an incident requires Federal coordination and is expected to be of long duration (e.g., weeks or months) or when the incident affects a large area of the country.

Unified Command is an Incident Command System application used when more than one agency has incident jurisdiction or when incidents cross political jurisdictions. Agencies work together through the designated members of the Unified Command, often the senior persons from agencies and/or disciplines participating in the Unified Command, to establish a common set of objectives and strategies and a single Incident Action Plan.

Area Command is an organization established to oversee the management of multiple incidents that are each being handled by a separate Incident Command System organization or to oversee the management of a very large or evolving incident that has multiple Incident Management Teams engaged. An Agency Administrator/Executive or other public official with jurisdictional responsibility for the incident usually makes the decision to establish an Area Command. An Area Command is activated only if necessary, depending on the complexity of the incident and incident management span-of-control considerations.

Types of JICs

Given the need for real-time communications, JICs can be organized in many ways, depending on the nature of the incident. Scroll down to review the different types of JICs.

Incident	• Optimal physical location for local and Incident Commander-assigned Public Information Officers to co-locate. • Easy media access is paramount to success.
Virtual	• Established when physical co-location is not feasible. • Incorporates technology and communication protocols.
Satellite	• Smaller in scale than other JICs. • Established primarily to support the incident JIC. • Operates under the control of the primary JIC for that incident. • Is not independent of that direction.
Area	• Supports wide-area multiple-incident ICS structures. • Could be established on a local or statewide basis. • Media access is paramount.
Support	• Established to support several incident JICs in multiple States. • Offers supplemental staff and resources outside of the disaster area.
National	• Established for long-duration incidents. • Established to support Federal response activities. • Staffed by numerous Federal departments and/or agencies. • Media access is paramount.

Lessons Learned: Virtual JICs

The establishment of a full-fledged JIC might not be an option during some incidents. For example, there may be a shortage of space, time limitations, or traffic issues hindering essential personnel from traveling. These problems may require the creation of a virtual JIC.

Former Virginia Governor Mark Warner's staff commented on the benefits of a virtual JIC in the National Capital Region (NCR):

> "We will work in partnership to develop a virtual Joint Information System for the NCR during response to a major emergency or disaster event. Although co-location may not be possible, creating a process and protocols for operating as a 'virtual' Joint Information Center will achieve the goal of a coordinated voice for the public and the media. In turn, an NCR policy about communicating risk and emergency protective measures to the public in the event of an attack will be jointly developed."

Understanding the Process

The process of getting information to the public during an incident is an ongoing cycle that involves four steps:

- Gathering information.
- Verifying information.
- Coordinating information.
- Disseminating information.

Let's look closer at each of these steps.

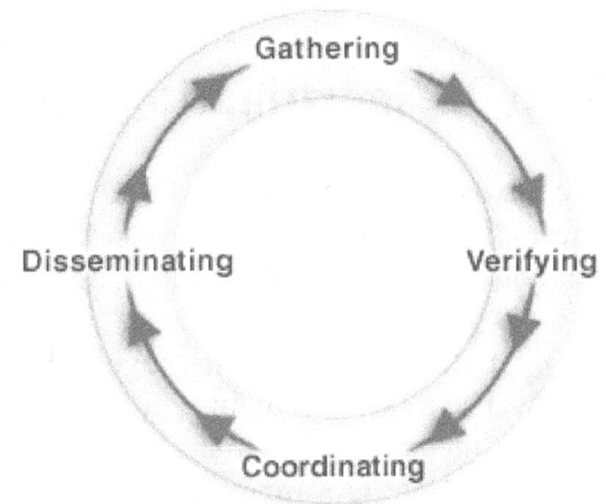

Step 1: Gathering Information

The first step in the process of getting information to the public during an incident is information gathering. Information is collected from:

- **Field PIOs,** who report to the JIC what they are observing and hearing in the field from the news media and the public.
- **Field Command,** a source of ongoing, official information on the response effort.
- **Public Inquiry Center,** a valuable source of information on the public's concerns and any misunderstandings or rumors that are surfacing.
- **Media monitoring,** which is used to assess the accuracy and content of news media reports. It also helps to identify trends and breaking issues.
- **News media,** a valuable source of developing information and current issues.

Step 2: Verifying Information

The next step in the process is to verify the accuracy of the information that has been collected, by consulting:

- **Other PIOs in the JIC.** Comparing notes—especially with the lead PIO and PIOs who are liaisons to the various program areas—is one way to verify the accuracy of information.
- **EOC sources,** including program leads, who should be asked to confirm information.
- **PIOs in the field.** Field PIOs are a valuable source for making sure what is reported to the EOC rings true with what they are learning from the news media and people in the field.

Step 3: Coordinating Information

The next step in the process is to coordinate with other PIOs who are part of the JIS. These PIOs include both those represented in the JIC and those working from another location who are part of the JIS. Coordinating information involves:

- **Establishing key message(s)** by prioritizing information to get out to the public. The mission remains getting the right information to the right people at the right time so they can make the right decisions.
- **Obtaining approval/clearance** from those in authority to ensure that the information is accurate, complete, and current. The approval process should be streamlined, however, to ensure that the information is released in a timely manner. This streamlined process should be addressed during planning and preparation.

Step 4: Disseminating Information

The next step in the process is to disseminate the information to the public. This step involves:

- **Using multiple methods.** In an emergency you may not have many options. Phone calls and interviews might be your primary means of getting information to the news media. You can support other efforts to get information out—such as community meetings and briefings—by providing talking points and flyers to field PIOs.
- **Monitoring the media.** Media monitoring is invaluable for ensuring that your message was understood by the news media and reported accurately and

completely to the public. Address important inaccuracies before they are reported incorrectly a second time.

An Evolving Situation

The process of getting information to the public will evolve as an incident becomes dynamic.

Imagine an incident that begins with a small accident involving a public bus. The initial reaction involves typical emergency actions to ensure public safety.

The response evolves and becomes more complex as it is revealed that the driver lost consciousness after exhibiting flu-like symptoms and several passengers were also exhibiting symptoms. Public health now becomes involved, a local EOC is activated and a JIC established, and the investigation intensifies.

Let's look at how the process of getting information to the public will have changed along with the situation.

	Initial Response: PIO will . . .	**Situation Escalated; EOC Activated: JIC will . . .**
STEP 1: Gathering Information	• Ask responders on-scene, call other sources as needed. • Observe news media coverage for accuracy of reporting and rumors.	• Have access to the scene (Field PIOs and Incident Command). • Ask EOC staff. • Ask Public Inquiry Center staff (if activated). • Attend regular briefings. • Use reports issued by communications and information management. • Observe news media coverage for accuracy of reporting and rumors.
STEP 2: Verifying Information	• Consult with Incident Command.	• Consult with other PIOs in the JIC.

		• Consult with other sources in the EOC. • Consult PIOs in the field. • Consult other PIOs in the JIS but not working out of the JIC.
STEP 3: Coordinating Information	• Get approval of Incident Command (verbal okay).	• Coordinate with other PIOs in the JIS to identify key messages. • Use prescribed protocol; use additional review as needed and as time allows. • Document the process.
STEP 4: Disseminating Information	• Primarily respond to reporters' questions and give interviews. • Distribute pre-scripted information such as backgrounders or factsheets, if possible.	• Schedule media briefings. • Give interviews (face-to-face; phone). • Arrange news conferences with multiple spokespersons. • Issue news releases—based on templates and unique to the incident (distributed electronically and by other means). • Use other technology as appropriate.

Typical JIC Functions and Organization

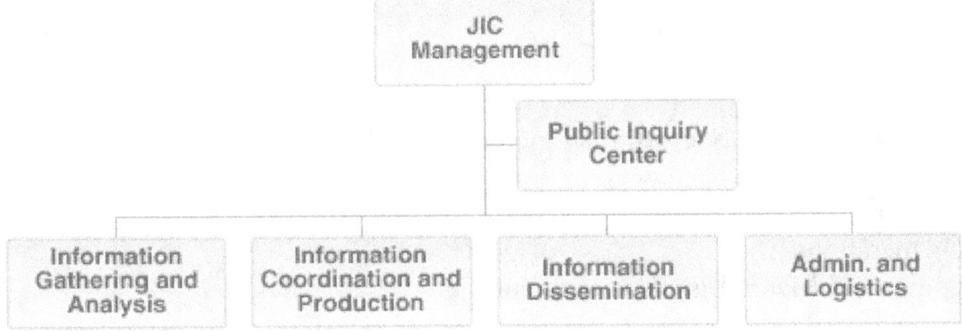

The JIC will be staffed and configured to meet the needs of the incident. Regardless of the number of PIOs and the scope of the operation, the JIC will be organized so that it can effectively get information to the public.

The JIC Organizational Elements

The **JIC Management Section** may include the positions of lead Public Information Officer (PIO), deputy lead PIO, and JIC coordinator. Typical functions for these positions are described below:

- The lead PIO's primary functions are to advise Incident Command on matters related to public information and to direct the overall public information effort. The lead PIO also manages the Joint Information Center (JIC).
- The deputy lead PIO assists the lead PIO to ensure that all JIC functions are operating efficiently. As directed, the deputy lead represents the lead PIO as needed and assumes responsibilities of the lead PIO as assigned.
- The JIC coordinator supervises daily operations of the JIC, executing plans and policies as directed by the lead/deputy lead PIOs. The JIC coordinator provides direction and support to JIC staff to ensure that all functions are operating efficiently and establishes internal communications procedures.

If necessary, a **Public Inquiry Center** (PIC) will be activated to respond directly to questions from the public using trained operators and under the direction of the lead PIO. The PIC serves a dual purpose: It disseminates information by responding to requests from the public, and it gathers information by identifying trends, inaccurate information, misunderstandings, or misperceptions reported by the public or reflected by their inquiries.

The **Information Gathering and Analysis Section** may include the following functions:

- News Analysis and Media Monitoring
- PIO Liaison Operations

The **Information Coordination and Production Section** may include the following functions:

- Research and Writing
- Photo Documentation
- Graphics and Production

The **Information Dissemination Section** may include the following functions:

- Media Relations
- Field PIO Operations
- Demographics and Media List Development

The **Administration and Logistics Section** includes the JIC administrative support function.

Lessons Learned: Katrina Case Example – Harris County, Texas

Following Katrina, Harris County, TX, organized an unprecedented coalition of local, State, and Federal agencies, along with nonprofit entities and nearly 60,000 volunteers, "to provide temporary shelter, social services, and relocation options" for the citizens in need of care.

A Joint Information Center (JIC) was established with representatives who are designated to handle public information from agencies and organizations involved in the event.

The JIC was responsible for media credentialing, media monitoring, managing celebrity visits, staffing phone banks, and publishing Web information. The JIC's dedicated Web site received more than 250,000 visitors in 20 days.

JIC Documentation

The Administration and Logistics section of the JIC is largely responsible for the documentation of JIC activities and products. Documentation includes:

- Draft, revised, and final news releases and Public Service Announcements (PSAs)
- Approval records (sign-offs) of all products
- Media contact logs
- Newsclips
- Videos of televised interviews and other coverage

- Photographs
- Copies of all products (talking points, backgrounders, briefing booklets, news conference agendas, flyers, etc.)
- Staffing information (contact information, assignments)
- Copies of legal notices

Lesson 6: Post-Incident Activities

Lesson Overview

This lesson will focus on how to benefit from experience and be ready for the next incident. At the end of this lesson, you should be able to:

- Describe methods to assess and analyze public information during and after an incident.
- Identify solutions that target and mitigate deficiencies in public information preparedness.
- Describe the process of replenishing public information resources.
- Describe strategies for maintaining the readiness of public information assets.

Assessing Your Operation

After an incident you should evaluate the effectiveness of your public information protocols and procedures so you can improve for the next incident.

After an incident you will want to determine:

1. What did we do this time?
2. What do we want to do the next time?
3. What do we need to do **now** to be ready for next time?

Step 1: What Did We Do This Time?

Part of assessing what you did is asking questions such as:

- How quickly/smoothly did you activate the Joint Information Center (JIC)?
- Did people get the right information?
- Was the information that was disseminated accurate?
- Was the information easy to understand?
- Was the information timely?

Other questions you will want to ask include:

- Did the right people get the information? Was the information accessible by people with language differences, hearing impairments, and other access and functional needs?
- Were there any issues of miscommunication or confusion? How were they caused and how were they resolved?
- Did you effectively support response/recovery?
- Did you work effectively with the news media?

Who Do You Ask?

To get a complete picture you will want feedback from:

- Incident Command
- Public Information Officers (PIOs) in the JIC
- PIOs in the field
- Other agency PIOs
- Public Inquiry Center
- News media (including editors)
- Other organizations within the multiagency coordination system
- The public (through community meetings)

Reviewing Documentation

Review your work products and other documentation and ask yourself, "Did we get the right information out to the right people at the right time?" Look at such things as:

- Media contact logs
- Newsclips
- Videos of televised interviews and other coverage
- News releases
- Copies of all products (talking points, briefing booklets, news conference agendas, flyers, etc.)

Internal Operations

Remember also to assess the internal workings of the JIC. If you ask staff to complete an after-action report, look at what they had to say about their role in the operation. Ask questions of staff in the JIC, such as:

- Did you have the equipment you needed?
- What were you lacking?
- Did you have the information you needed?
- Did the approval process work?
- Did you feel your skills were utilized?

Step 2: What Do We Want To Do the Next Time?

After you have determined what you did, the next step is to decide what you want to do differently the next time. Look at successes that you want to replicate and the problems you want to avoid repeating.

Set goals for the next time:

- **Output.** What products will you produce? What quality will you accept?
- **Systems issues.** How do you want to operate?
- **Logistical factors.** What equipment, technology, and environment do you want in your JIC?
- **Human factors.** What human resources do you want? Consider skills and staffing level. What comfort, security, and safety issues will you want to have under control?

Step 3: What Do We Need To Do Now To Be Ready?

Focusing on your goals for the next time, select a strategy for improving in each key area.

To Improve Output:

- Provide training to improve PIO skills (e.g., writing, on-camera interview techniques, and photography).
- Rewrite pre-scripted news releases and factsheets so they are current.
- Add to your Smart Book.

To Improve Systems:

- Streamline processes that slowed you down (e.g., approval, production, dissemination).
- Institutionalize into the standard operating procedures those processes that contributed to your success (e.g., alternative dissemination process).

To Improve Logistical Factors:

- Identify equipment that could help you be more effective.
- Research new technology that will improve operations.
- Research costs and other factors for consideration during the appropriate budget cycle.

To Improve Human Factors:

- Ensure that your standard operating procedures and training address personal comfort, security, and safety.
- Update your records to ensure you are tapping the skills of all PIOs.
- Identify gaps in skills and recruit to fill those gaps.

Taking Stock

Facilities, equipment, and supplies are an important part of any public information operation. After an incident you will need to inventory and replenish resources.

Experienced and trained PIOs are probably your greatest resource. If you are relying on part-time, disaster employee, or volunteer PIOs to meet incident requirements you may need to regularly recruit qualified individuals.

After an incident interest in the community will be high. Use this time as an opportunity to speak with college students, retirees, and service organizations to line up possible adjunct PIOs for the next incident.

Financial Reporting

Provide your finance department with data on the costs of running the JIC during the incident (including overtime and incidentals like cab fare). Become familiar with local, State, and Federal reimbursement guidelines.

Maintaining the System

You may have gathered up-to-date contact information in the course of the incident response. Immediately after the incident—when the information is fresh in your mind—update your news media, PIO, and other contact information.

Update your plan and procedures to reflect lessons learned. Distribute plan revisions to staff, other agency PIOs, and other components of the emergency response team.

Incorporate any changes in your training.

www.ingramcontent.com/pod-product-compliance
Lightning Source LLC
Chambersburg PA
CBHW081853250726
48659CB00008B/2730